UNITED STATES COURT OF APPEALS
FOR THE NINTH CIRCUIT

TARLA MAKAEFF, on behalf of herself and all others similarly situated, *Plaintiff-counter-defendant-Appellant,* and BRANDON KELLER; ED OBERKROM; PATRICIA MURPHY, *Plaintiffs,* v. TRUMP UNIVERSITY, LLC, a New York limited liability company, AKA Trump Entrepreneur Initiative, *Defendant-counter-claimant-Appellee,* and DONALD J. TRUMP, *Defendant.*	No. 11-55016 D.C. No. 3:10-cv-00940-IEG-WVG OPINION

Appeal from the United States District Court
for the Southern District of California
Irma E. Gonzalez, Chief District Judge, Presiding

Argued and Submitted
January 18, 2012—Irvine, California

Filed April 17, 2013

Before: Alex Kozinski, Chief Judge, Kim McLane
Wardlaw and Richard A. Paez, Circuit Judges.

Opinion by Judge Wardlaw;
Concurrence by Chief Judge Kozinski;
Concurrence by Judge Paez

SUMMARY[*]

California Anti-SLAPP Statute / Defamation

The panel reversed the district court's denial of a pre-trial
motion to strike a counterclaim pursuant to California's anti-
SLAPP statute, and remanded for further proceedings.

A disgruntled former customer sued Trump University for
deceptive business practices, and Trump University
counterclaimed for defamation. The district court held that
Trump University was not a public figure, and denied the

---

[*] This summary constitutes no part of the opinion of the court. It has
been prepared by court staff for the convenience of the reader.

motion to strike the defamation claim under the Anti-SLAPP (Strategic Lawsuits Against Public Participation) statute.

The panel held that Trump University was a limited public figure with respect to the subject of its advertising, and to prevail on its defamation claim, must demonstrate that the customer acted with actual malice.

Chief Judge Kozinski, joined by Judge Paez, concurred. He believes that *United States ex rel. Newsham v. Lockheed Missiles & Spice Co.*, 190 F.3d 963 (9th Cir. 1999), is wrong and should be reconsidered.

Judge Paez, joined by Chief Judge Kozinski, concurred. He believes that *United States ex rel. Newsham v. Lockheed Missiles & Spice Co.*, 190 F.3d 963 (9th Cir. 1999), is wrong and should be reconsidered. Judge Paez stated that another reason to reconsider the application of state anti-SLAPP statutes in federal court is that there are significant state-by-state variations within the circuit.

COUNSEL

Eric Alan Isaacson (argued), Rachel L. Jensen, Amanda M. Frame, and Thomas R. Merrick, Robbins Geller Rudman & Dowd LLP, San Diego, California; Amber L. Eck, Zeldes & Haeggquist, LLP, San Diego, California, for Plaintiff-Counter-Defendant-Appellant.

Jill A. Martin (argued), Rancho Palos Verdes, California; David Keith Schneider, Yunker & Schneider, San Diego, California, for Defendant-Counter-Claimant-Appellee.

Christopher M. Burke, Scott & Scott LLP, San Diego, California, for Amicus Curiae Consumer Attorneys of California.

David Blair-Loy, ACLU Foundation of San Diego & Imperial Counties, San Diego, California, for Amicus Curiae American Civil Liberties Union of San Diego & Imperial Counties.

OPINION

WARDLAW, Circuit Judge:

No one would deny that Donald Trump, the real estate magnate, television personality, author, and erstwhile presidential candidate, cuts a celebrated, if controversial, public figure. We must decide whether Trump University, LLC, a private, for-profit entity purporting to teach Trump's "insider success secrets," is itself a public or limited public figure so as to implicate the First Amendment. Disgruntled former customer Tarla Makaeff sued Trump University for, among other things, deceptive business practices. In return, Trump University counterclaimed against Makaeff for defamation. Makaeff moved to strike the defamation claim, contending that Trump University is a public figure and therefore must show that she made her allegedly defamatory statements with "actual malice," a requirement she contends Trump University cannot prove. *See New York Times Co. v. Sullivan*, 376 U.S. 254 (1964). Denying the motion to strike, the district court held that Trump University is not a public figure. We disagree. Trump University is a limited public figure, and, to prevail here, must demonstrate that Makaeff acted with actual malice. Because the district court erred by failing to recognize Trump University's status as a limited public figure, we reverse and remand for further proceedings.

I.

Donald Trump founded Trump University[1] because he has "a real passion for learning." Trump, who describes himself as Trump University's chairman, portrays the venture as the next step in his progression from real estate tycoon to educator. "My books and seminars have always included a strong educational or 'lessons learned' slant. . . . [Trump University] grew out of my desire to impart my business knowledge, accumulated over the years, and my realization that there is a huge demand for practical, convenient education that teaches success." So born, Trump University took shape as a limited liability company offering real estate seminars and other training programs to would-be real estate investors. Its stated mission is to "train, educate and mentor entrepreneurs on achieving financial independence through real estate investing."

A.

Trump University has not been shy about touting its connection to its eponymous creator. Evoking Trump's well-known reality television series, Trump University's advertisements promise that enrolling in Trump University is

---

[1] After this action was filed, Trump University changed its name to "The Trump Entrepreneur Initiative" because New York State Department of Education officials objected to the corporation's use of the term "University." *See* Michael Barbaro, *New York Attorney General is Investigating Trump's For-Profit School*, N.Y. Times, May 20, 2011, at A18. For purposes of continuity, we use the name Trump University.

"the next best thing to being [Trump's] Apprentice." Its advertisements prominently showcase Trump's photo while urging consumers to "[l]earn from the Master," and promising to teach Trump's "insider success secrets." The home page of Trump University's website features Trump's photo next to the words: "Are YOU My Next Apprentice? Prove it to me!" Trump University students are shown a slide depicting Trump University as the latest of Donald Trump's achievements, alongside such feats as buying the "Taj Mahal" casino in Atlantic City and completing the "Trump Tower" in Manhattan.

Trump University has collaborated with Donald Trump on several books.[2] It holds the copyright in the books *Trump 101*, written by Donald Trump with Meredith McIver, *see* Donald J. Trump, *Trump 101: The Way to Success* (2007) ("*Trump 101*"), and *Wealth Building 101, see Wealth Building 101: Your First 90 Days on the Path to Prosperity* (Donald J. Trump, ed. 2007) ("*Wealth Building 101*"). Both works tout Trump's involvement with Trump University. For instance, in his Foreword to *Trump 101*, Michael Sexton, the president of Trump University, asserts that Donald Trump "has made the decision to become an educator himself, through his public appearances, *The Apprentice*, his books, and now, Trump University." Michael Sexton, *Foreword* to

---

[2] We grant Makaeff's requests to take notice of book collaborations between Donald Trump and Trump University, newspaper and magazine articles, and web pages. *See* Fed. R. Evid. 201; *Von Saher v. Norton Simon Museum of Art at Pasadena*, 592 F.3d 954, 960 (9th Cir. 2010) (holding that it is proper to take judicial notice of various publications introduced "to indicate what was in the public realm at the time, not whether the contents of those articles were in fact true") (internal quotation marks and citation omitted).

Trump 101, at xiv. In the Foreword to *Wealth Building 101*, president Sexton asserts that

> [o]ther organizations try to sell help alone, without the proven expertise to back it up, and just when you begin to realize that the advice you paid for is unproven and ineffective—they try to sell you more expensive products. They hook you on promises and never deliver.
>
> Neither I nor our chairman, Donald J. Trump, would stand for that at Trump University.

Michael Sexton, *Foreword* to *Wealth Building 101*, at ix.

Almost from its inception, Trump University drew public comment. Donald Trump referenced the attention in 2005, noting in a blog post on the Trump University website that the nationally syndicated comic strip "Doonesbury" spent a week lampooning "the disparity between [Trump University] and a traditional university." The post was entitled: "We're laughing all the way to the bank."[3] By 2007, however, disappointed customers had begun posting complaints about Trump University on Internet message boards. Some posts alleged that Trump University programs were "scams" that focused on "upselling" customers to more expensive seminars and workshops. In late 2007, an investigative article by journalist David Lazarus of the Los Angeles Times

---

[3] The post also noted that Trump University had been mocked in one of television host Jay Leno's monologues and the New York Post's Page Six cartoon.

questioned Trump University's business practices in the larger context of the subprime mortgage crisis. *See* David Lazarus, *Trump Spins in Foreclosure Game*, L.A. Times, at C1, December 12, 2007. The column quoted Donald Trump ("I love helping people") and described a satisfied Trump University customer ("I have control of four properties"), but also cited the skepticism of real estate experts over "push[ing] neophytes to take such risks" in the burgeoning foreclosure market.[4] *Id.*

B.

In August 2008, Tarla Makaeff attended Trump University's three-day "Fast Track to Foreclosure Workshop" at a cost of approximately $1,495, which Makaeff says she split with a friend. Makaeff describes the seminars as slick productions featuring carefully choreographed presentations, speakers blaring "For the Love of Money," the theme song from Trump's hit reality television series "The Apprentice," and Trump University representatives exhorting customers to raise their credit card limits, ostensibly to enable "real estate transactions," but actually to facilitate the purchase of the $34,995 "Trump Gold Elite Program."

Apparently persuaded, Makaeff paid $34,995 to enroll in the Gold Elite Program, which entitled her to four three-day "advanced training workshops," a three-day "mentoring session in the field," and "training publications, software, and

---

[4] Four days later, the Los Angeles Times ran a follow-up piece by the same journalist, recounting a phone conversation he enjoyed with an irate Donald Trump following publication of the first column. *See* David Lazarus, *Trump's a Grump About Column on His 'Priceless' Tips*, L.A. Times, at C1, December 16, 2007.

other materials." Makaeff's satisfaction with the program was short-lived. In April 2009, after completing five more programs and workshops, and after seven months of the Gold Elite Program, she wrote an email to Trump University complaining that she was in a "precarious financial position" and that she "did not receive the value that I thought I would for such a large expenditure." Makaeff had earlier spoken by phone with a Trump University representative who had told her that she was ineligible for a refund of the cost of the program. In response to Makaeff's email, Trump University offered more free "mentoring services," which Makaeff accepted.

By Fall 2009, however, the relationship between Makaeff and Trump University had gone irretrievably south. Makaeff wrote to her bank and the Better Business Bureau, contacted government agencies, and posted on Internet message boards about her dispute with Trump University. Makaeff requested a refund of $5,100 from her bank for services charged for Trump University programs. In the letter to the Better Business Bureau, Makaeff requested a refund of her payments for services that she did not receive. In both letters, Makaeff asserted that Trump University engaged in "fraudulent business practices," "deceptive business practices," "illegal predatory high pressure closing tactics," "personal financial information fraud," "illegal bait and switch," "brainwashing scheme[s]," "outright fraud," "grand larceny," "identity theft," "unsolicited taking of personal credit and trickery into [sic] opening credit cards," "fraudulent business practices utilized for illegal material gain," "felonious teachings," "neurolinguistic programming and high pressure sales tactics based on the psychology of scarcity," "unethical tactics," "a gargantuan amount of misleading, fraudulent, and predatory behavior," and business practices that are "criminal." Trump University claims that Makaeff published similar statements to unknown third parties and to the general public on the Internet.

In April 2010, Makaeff filed a class action complaint against Trump University, accusing it of, among other things, deceptive business practices. Trump University counterclaimed against Makaeff for defamation based on the statements in her letters and Internet postings. Thereafter, Makaeff moved under California's "anti-SLAPP" law, California Code of Civil Procedure § 425.16, to strike the defamation claim, a motion the district court denied. While it held that Trump University's suit arose from protected conduct under the anti-SLAPP statute, the court concluded that Trump University had demonstrated a reasonable probability of prevailing on the merits of its defamation claim, and therefore dismissal of that claim under the anti-SLAPP statute was not warranted.

II.

California law provides for the pre-trial dismissal of certain actions, known as Strategic Lawsuits Against Public Participation, or SLAPPs, that "'masquerade as ordinary lawsuits'" but are intended to deter ordinary people "from exercising their political or legal rights or to punish them for doing so." *Batzel v. Smith*, 333 F.3d 1018, 1024 (9th Cir. 2003) (quoting *Wilcox v. Superior Court*, 33 Cal. Rptr. 2d 446, 450 (Ct. App. 1994)). We have jurisdiction to review the district court's denial of Makaeff's anti-SLAPP motion under the collateral order doctrine. *See Hilton v. Hallmark Cards*, 599 F.3d 894, 900 & n.2 (9th Cir. 2010); *see also Vess v. Ciba-Geigy Corp. USA*, 317 F.3d 1097, 1109 (9th Cir. 2003) ("Motions to strike a state law claim under California's anti-SLAPP statute may be brought in federal court."). We review de novo the district court's determination of a motion to strike under California's anti-SLAPP statute. *Vess*, 317 F.3d at 1102; *Gilbert v. Sykes*, 53 Cal. Rptr. 3d 752, 760 (Ct. App. 2007).

III.

California's anti-SLAPP statute allows a defendant to file a "special motion to strike" to dismiss an action before trial. Cal. Civ. Proc. Code § 425.16. To prevail on an anti-SLAPP motion, the moving defendant must make a prima facie showing that the plaintiff's suit arises from an act in furtherance of the defendant's constitutional right to free speech. *Batzel*, 333 F.3d at 1024. The burden then shifts to the plaintiff, here Trump University, to establish a reasonable probability that it will prevail on its claim in order for that claim to survive dismissal. Cal. Civ. Proc. Code § 425.16(b)(1); *Gilbert*, 53 Cal. Rptr. 3d at 760. Under this standard, the claim should be dismissed if the plaintiff presents an insufficient legal basis for it, or if, on the basis of the facts shown by the plaintiff, "no reasonable jury could find for the plaintiff." *Metabolife Int'l, Inc. v. Wornick*, 264 F.3d 832, 840 (9th Cir. 2001) (citation and internal quotation marks omitted).

In evaluating Makaeff's anti-SLAPP motion, the district court held that Makaeff had met her initial burden of showing that Trump University's claim arose from an act by Makaeff in furtherance of her free speech rights. Proceeding to the second step, the court concluded that Trump University had established a reasonable probability of success on the merits of the defamation claim. In particular, it held that Trump University was not a public figure under *Gertz v. Robert*

Welch, Inc., 418 U.S. 323, 345 (1974), and Trump University therefore did not need to meet the heightened standard of proof for defamation established in *New York Times Co. v. Sullivan*, 376 U.S. 254 (1964). Under this heightened standard, Trump University would have been required to show that Makaeff made her statements with actual malice. *Gertz*, 418 U.S. at 342.

A.

The district court was correct that Makaeff met her initial burden of showing that Trump University's defamation claim arose from an act in furtherance of her free speech rights. *Vess*, 317 F.3d at 1110. Under California's anti-SLAPP statute, such acts must be "in connection with a public issue," and include:

> (1) any written or oral statement or writing made before a legislative, executive, or judicial proceeding, or any other official proceeding authorized by law,

> (2) any written or oral statement or writing made in connection with an issue under consideration or review by a legislative, executive, or judicial body, or any other official proceeding authorized by law,

> (3) any written or oral statement or writing made in a place open to the public or a public forum in connection with an issue of public interest, or

> (4) any other conduct in furtherance of the exercise of the constitutional right of petition or the constitutional right of free speech in connection with a public issue or an issue of public interest.

Cal. Civ. Proc. Code § 425.16(e). The district court determined that Makaeff's statements fell into the fourth category, conduct in connection "with a public issue or an issue of public interest," because the statements provided "consumer protection information."

Under California law, statements warning consumers of fraudulent or deceptive business practices constitute a topic of widespread public interest, so long as they are provided in the context of information helpful to consumers. For instance, in *Wilbanks v. Wolk*, 17 Cal. Rptr. 3d 497 (Ct. App. 2004), Gloria Wolk, a consumer advocate and expert on viatical settlements (arrangements in which dying persons sell their life insurance policies to investors to help pay for medical care and other expenses), posted negative comments on her website about a certain broker of such settlements. *Id.* at 499, 507. The California Court of Appeal held that the statements were protected activity under the anti-SLAPP statute because they were "consumer protection information." *Id.* at 507. It reasoned:

> The statements made by [the defendant] were not simply a report of one broker's business practices, of interest only to that broker and to those who had been affected by those practices. [The defendant's] statements were a warning not to use plaintiffs' services. In the context of information ostensibly provided

> to aid consumers choosing among brokers, the statements, therefore, were directly connected to an issue of public concern.

Id. at 507–08.

Similarly, in *Paradise Hills Associates v. Procel*, 1 Cal. Rptr. 2d 514 (Ct. App. 1991), the California Court of Appeal held that a disgruntled buyer's statements made against a seller were protected by the First Amendment. *Id.* at 523. There, a homeowner embroiled in a dispute with a residential developer posted signs on her house, spoke with reporters, distributed leaflets, and spoke to prospective customers to urge them not to buy houses from the developer. *Id.* at 516. The developer sued, arguing that the homeowner's statements were not protected by the First Amendment because they "relate solely to her private concerns." *Id.* at 522. Rejecting that argument, the court reasoned that consumers have an "'interest in matters which affect their roles as consumers.'" *Id.* (quoting *Concerned Consumers League v. O'Neill*, 371 F. Supp. 644, 648 (E.D. Wis. 1974)). The court therefore held that the First Amendment protected the homeowner's statements. *Id.* at 523.

Here, according to Trump University's defamation counterclaim, Makaeff published statements to "unknown third parties and the general public on the Internet."[5] Makaeff

---

[5] Trump University's appellate briefing omits any mention of Makaeff's Internet postings, limiting its arguments to the statements found in Makaeff's letters. However, California's anti-SLAPP statute instructs the court to base its determination on the "pleadings" and "affidavits" of the parties. Cal. Civ. Proc. Code § 425.16(b)(2). Trump University's pleadings and the declarations of Makaeff and Trump University president Michael Sexton reference the Internet postings. Moreover, the district

claims she posted these statements "to alert other consumers of my opinions and experience with Trump University," and to "inform other consumers of my opinion that Trump University did not deliver what it promised." Her explanation is plausible. Makaeff's letter to her bank suggests that she spoke out with the goal of stopping Trump University from defrauding other consumers:

> I am contacting the Better Business Bureau (BBB), the Federal Trade Commission (FTC), Bureau of Consumer Protection and the FDIC as well as posting the facts of my highly negative experience on a wide variety of Internet sites to ensure that this organization at some point is stopped from defrauding others with its predatory behavior. I am also contacting the media to give them a statement of facts so that they can expose this scam and am willing to go to whatever lengths necessary to obtain my money back including taking legal action at the state and federal levels for this crime that has been committed to [sic] thousands of students nationwide who have been preyed on and victimized as I know I am one of many.

Makaeff's posts on anonymous third-party websites could not have resolved her private dispute with Trump University. We therefore conclude that the postings constituted consumer

---

court referenced those Internet postings in the order denying Makaeff's motion. We are therefore satisfied that Trump University's counterclaim "aris[es]," at least in part, from Makaeff's Internet postings to anonymous third parties. Cal. Civ. Proc. Code § 425.16(b)(1).

protection information because they were intended as "a warning not to use plaintiffs' services" and came in the context of information that was "provided to aid consumers."[6] *Wilbanks*, 17 Cal. Rptr. 3d at 508.

Moreover, we have doubts about Trump University's claim that Makaeff wrote her letters to her bank and the Better Business Bureau with purely private motives. The Better Business Bureau identifies its mission as advancing trust in the marketplace by offering objective and unbiased information about businesses to consumers.[7] Therefore, the statements Makaeff made in her letter to the Bureau, even if made in the context of a request that it intercede in her dispute with Trump University, are not so easily separated from "information . . . provided to aid consumers." *Id.*

Because at least some of Makaeff's statements were made with the intent to warn consumers about the educational experience at Trump University, we agree with the district court that Trump University's counterclaim arises from an act protected under the anti-SLAPP statute.

B.

Because Trump University's counterclaim arose from an act protected under the anti-SLAPP statute, the burden shifts

---

[6] In her declaration supporting her motion to strike, Makaeff asserts that she contacted the Attorney General of New York, Federal Trade Commission, Federal Bureau of Investigation, New York State Board of Education, New York Bureau of Consumer Protection, and New York District Attorney Special Prosecutors Bureau regarding Trump University.

[7] *See Vision, Mission and Values*, BBB, http://www.bbb.org/us/mission-and-values/ (last visited Mar. 22, 2013).

to Trump University to show a reasonable probability of prevailing on the merits of its claim. *Metabolife Int'l*, 264 F.3d at 840. Trump University's claim is for defamation, "an invasion of the interest in reputation." *Gilbert*, 53 Cal. Rptr. 3d at 764. Under California law, defamation is "'the intentional publication of a statement of fact which is false, unprivileged, and has a natural tendency to injure or which causes special damage.'" *Id.* (quoting *Ringler Assocs., Inc. v. Md. Cas. Co.*, 96 Cal. Rptr. 2d 136, 148 (Ct. App. 2000)). Before we address Trump University's specific allegations to determine whether it has met its burden, we must first decide (1) whether Makaeff's speech is protected by California's litigation privilege, and (2) whether Trump University is a "public figure."

1.

If Makaeff's statements lie within California's statutory litigation privilege, then Trump University has no probability of success on the merits and Makaeff's special motion to strike should have been granted. California Civil Code section 47(b) renders privileged, inter alia, any publication of a statement made in a judicial proceeding, or "in the initiation or course of any other proceeding authorized by law," with some specific exceptions. Cal. Civ. Code § 47(b). "[T]he privilege applies to any communication (1) made in judicial or quasi-judicial proceedings; (2) by litigants or other participants authorized by law; (3) to achieve the objects of the litigation; and (4) that have some connection or logical relation to the action." *Silberg v. Anderson*, 786 P.2d 365, 369 (Cal. 1990). The privilege also applies to a communication related to an *anticipated* lawsuit, if it is preliminary to an imminent proposed lawsuit contemplated in good faith and the purpose of the proposed litigation is to resolve the dispute. *Edwards v. Centex Real Estate Corp.*, 61 Cal. Rptr. 2d 518, 530–31 (Ct. App. 1997).

The district court correctly concluded that Makaeff's statements are not protected by California's section 47(b) litigation privilege. Makaeff cannot assert the privilege on the basis that her statements were made in advance of an anticipated lawsuit. Makaeff's letters make no statement more concrete than that she would be willing to go to any lengths, including legal action, to get back her money. Therefore, any lawsuit at the time she made her statements was nothing more than a mere possibility, not imminent proposed litigation. *Id.* at 530.

Moreover, Makaeff made her statements not in a judicial proceeding, but to a private bank, the Better Business Bureau, and to the general public on the Internet. Although California courts have extended the litigation privilege to quasi-judicial proceedings such as private commercial arbitration, *see, e.g., Moore v. Conliffe*, 871 P.2d 204, 219 (Cal. 1994), Makaeff was not actually in arbitration with Trump University, as she asserts. California courts have extended the litigation privilege to only formal arbitration or mediation proceedings to which the parties consented as an alternative to trial. *See, e.g., Howard v. Drapkin*, 271 Cal. Rptr. 893, 864 (Ct. App. 1990) (where plaintiff and ex-husband stipulated that an independent psychologist would serve as a neutral third party to perform dispute resolution services, the psychologist was entitled to protection for statements made during resulting proceeding). Trump University never consented to arbitration or mediation proceedings with Makaeff, her bank, or the Better Business Bureau.

2.

The next question we must answer is whether Trump University is a public figure under *New York Times Co. v. Sullivan*. If so, Trump University must demonstrate by clear and convincing evidence that Makaeff made her allegedly defamatory statements with "actual malice"; that is, "with knowledge of [their] falsity or with reckless disregard for the truth." *Gertz*, 418 U.S. at 328, 342. If, upon remand, Trump University cannot make such a showing, it has no possibility of success on the merits and the district court should grant Makaeff's special motion to strike.

In *Gertz*, the Supreme Court identified two types of public figures: (1) all purpose public figures, who occupy "positions of such persuasive power and influence that they are deemed public figures for all purposes," and (2) limited purpose public figures, who achieve their status by "thrust[ing] themselves to the forefront of particular public controversies in order to influence the resolution of the issues involved." *Id.* at 345. Because "[i]n either case such persons assume special prominence in the resolution of public questions," both categories of public figures are subject to the heightened burden of proof in defamation cases. *Id.* at 351.

The Court articulated two policy reasons for requiring public figures to show actual malice. First, public figures enjoy "greater access to the channels of effective communication" than private individuals, and are therefore better able to "contradict the lie or correct the error." *Id.* at 344. Second, the Court identified a normative consideration, rooted in the observation that public figures became such "by reason of the notoriety of their achievements or the vigor and success with which they seek the public's attention." *Id.* at

342. In other words, true public figures voluntarily assume positions of importance in society. Public speakers, the Court noted, were thus entitled to act on the assumption that such public figures had also willingly exposed themselves to the risk of injury from defamatory falsehood. *Id.* at 345.

a.

The district court correctly held that Trump University is not an all purpose public figure. "Absent clear evidence of general fame or notoriety in the community, and pervasive involvement in the affairs of society," an individual is not a public figure for all purposes. *Id.* at 352. The record does not support the conclusion that Trump University is generally famous or that it wields vast influence in public affairs. Makaeff argues that Trump University is a public figure because of its status as a "university." A handful of New York state cases have held that private colleges and universities are all purpose public figures, *see, e.g., Ithaca Coll. v. Yale Daily News Publ'g Co.*, 433 N.Y.S. 2d 530, 534 (App. Div. 1980), but those cases are inapposite. Trump University has little in common with the Ithaca Colleges of the world. As a private, for-profit entity offering real estate seminars to small groups of students, it possesses neither a large, diverse student body, nor "general fame or notoriety" in the community, both factors which the New York Supreme Court, Appellate Division, found dispositive in *Ithaca College*. *Id.* Indeed, Trump University more closely resembles the private computer programming school in *Commercial Programming Unlimited v. Columbia Broadcasting Systems, Inc.*, 367 N.Y.S. 2d 986, 992 (Sup. Ct. 1975), *rev'd on other grounds*, 378 N.Y.S. 2d 69 (App. Div. 1975), which the New York court concluded was not a public figure.

Makaeff and *amicus* ACLU Foundation of San Diego and Imperial Counties, Inc. also argue that Trump University is an all purpose public figure because it is inextricably intertwined with Donald Trump, who all parties agree is an all purpose public figure for First Amendment purposes. Makaeff and the ACLU contend that *père* Trump's public figure status should be imputed to Trump University. We find this argument unavailing. Makaeff cites for support an out-of-circuit district court opinion, *Schiavone Construction Co. v. Time., Inc.*, 619 F. Supp. 684 (D.N.J. 1985), which we do not find apposite. There, contractor Ronald Schiavone and his construction company brought a libel action against Time, Inc., over a magazine article that linked the name Schiavone to organized crime. *Id.* at 686–87. The court held in a footnote that if Schiavone was a public figure, then so was his company:

> Plaintiffs' status in this regard is identical one to the other. The court's holding that defamation of Schiavone Construction Co. may be "of and concerning" plaintiff Ronald Schiavone, simply because the two are inextricably intertwined by name and corporate structure, requires that if one is deemed a public figure so must the other be.

Id. at 704 n.13 (citation omitted).

In *Schiavone*, the court's holding was based on its earlier observation that Schiavone was the principal owner, chairman of the board of directors, CEO, and person "who might well have been responsible for the major decisions" of his construction company. *Id.* at 697. Although Donald Trump is the founder and chairman of Trump University, he is not so "inextricably intertwined" with Trump University's corporate structure and daily affairs as to in effect be the alter ego of the University, a showing *Schiavone* seems to require.[8]

b.

Because Trump University is not an all-purpose public figure, we examine the nature and extent of Trump University's "participation in the particular controversy giving rise to the defamation" to determine whether it is a public figure for the limited purposes of a defamation claim over its educational practices. *Gertz*, 418 U.S. at 352. In undertaking this inquiry, we consider whether (i) a public controversy existed when the statements were made, (ii) whether the alleged defamation is related to the plaintiff's participation in the controversy, and (iii) whether the plaintiff voluntarily injected itself into the controversy for the purpose of influencing the controversy's ultimate resolution. *Gilbert*, 53 Cal. Rptr. 3d at 762; *see also Gertz*, 418 U.S. at 351–52. The district court assumed without deciding that a public controversy existed regarding Trump University's business practices, but held that Trump University did nothing to voluntarily thrust itself into the controversy. We disagree with this holding.

---

[8] Trump University argues that because the district court in *Schiavone* made its holding in the context of determining whether the plaintiff was a limited purpose public figure, *see Schiavone*, 619 F. Supp at 702, that holding has no relevance to the question of whether Trump University is an all purpose public figure. Because we conclude that *Schiavone* is inapposite in any case, we do not address this argument.

i.

We have little difficulty in concluding that a public controversy existed over Trump University's educational and business practices when Makaeff made her statements about them. As Donald Trump himself admits on the Trump University website, Trump University provoked public attention nearly from the outset, much of it derisive. Of course, general interest in Donald Trump is not sufficient to create a public controversy. *Cf. Time, Inc. v. Firestone*, 424 U.S. 448, 454–55 (1976) ("[D]issolution of a marriage through judicial proceedings is not the sort of 'public controversy' referred to in *Gertz*."). Instead, a public controversy "must be a real dispute, the outcome of which affects the general public or some segment of it." *Waldbaum v. Fairchild Publ'ns*, 627 F.2d 1289, 1296 (D.C. Cir. 1980); *see also Annette F. v. Sharon S.*, 15 Cal. Rptr. 3d 100, 112 (Ct. App. 2004).

Here, any general interest in Trump University stemming from its celebrity founder soon ripened into an actual dispute over Trump University's business and educational practices. By 2007 and 2008, disgruntled Trump University customers were posting complaints on public Internet message boards. Also by 2007, a columnist for a mass market newspaper had begun to report on Trump University's educational practices and business model. *See* Lazarus, *Trump Spins in Foreclosure Game, supra.* The column describes a Trump University seminar in unflattering terms, quotes both supporters and detractors of Trump University's programs, and discusses Trump University's educational practices against the backdrop of the mortgage foreclosure crisis. *Id.* We therefore conclude that by Fall 2009, the "specific question" of Trump University's legitimacy had become a public controversy. *Waldbaum*, 627 F.2d at 1297.

Moreover, this dispute had the potential to affect "the general public or some segment of it in an appreciable way." *Id*. at 1296. Trump University's business model involved offering seminars that encouraged members of the public to participate in the market for foreclosed properties, which had grown substantially in the wake of the 2007 financial and mortgage crisis. These activities, carried out by Trump University and other purveyors of real estate investment advice, had the potential to affect local housing markets by increasing or decreasing real estate speculation in the market for foreclosed homes. The debate over Trump University's business practices thus held ramifications not just for Trump University and its customers, but for all participants in the local housing markets. *See id.* at 1299 (a public debate over the marketing policies of a cooperative supermarket held the potential to affect consumers and industry retailers in the surrounding area).

Thus, a public controversy existed over Trump University's business practices at the time Makaeff made her statements in Fall 2009.

ii.

The district court erroneously concluded that Trump University did not voluntarily inject itself into this public controversy. Under *Gertz*, Trump University must have "thrust [itself] to the forefront" of this particular controversy "in order to influence the resolution of the issues involved." 418 U.S. at 345. The district court concluded that even if Trump University was involved in the controversy over its allegedly deceptive business practices, its involvement was not voluntary. We disagree.

We hold, as have the Third and Fourth Circuits, that large scale, aggressive advertising can inject a person or entity into a public controversy that arises from the subject of that advertising. Advertising, conducted on a large scale and addressing or creating a public controversy, can be a way of "voluntarily expos[ing] [the company] to increased risk of injury from defamatory falsehood" concerning the company and its advertised products. *Id.* Moreover, entities that advertise aggressively "enjoy significantly greater access to the channels of effective communication and hence have a more realistic opportunity to counteract false statements then [sic] private individuals normally enjoy." *Id.* at 344.

In *Steaks Unlimited, Inc. v. Deaner*, 623 F.2d 264 (3d Cir. 1980), for instance, the Third Circuit considered a defamation suit against a television consumer affairs reporter for WTAE-TV in Pittsburgh, who was investigating a four-day steak-sale bonanza promoted by a company called Steaks Unlimited. She reported that the quality of the steaks was low and the prices high, and further stated that Steaks Unlimited's advertising was deceptive. *Id.* at 268. The Third Circuit held that Steaks Unlimited was a limited purpose public figure because of its "advertising blitz":

> Immediately upon its entry into the Pittsburgh area, Steaks launched an intensive campaign over local radio stations, through local newspapers, by large signs displayed at the sales locations and by handbills given to persons walking near Steaks Unlimited Sales locations at the various Zayre stores. The

advertising costs exceeded $16,000.00. Moreover, both WTAE-TV and the Bureau of Consumer Affairs received numerous telephone complaints from Pittsburgh area consumers, complaining about the poor quality of Steaks Unlimited's beef as well as (about) asserted misrepresentations as to the quality and type of beef being sold. Under these circumstances, the district court properly concluded that Steaks voluntarily injected itself into a matter of public interest—indeed, it appears to have created a controversy—for the purpose of influencing the consuming public. In short, through its advertising blitz, Steaks invited public attention, comment, and criticism.

Id. at 273–74 (internal quotation marks and footnotes omitted).[9] Similarly, the Fourth Circuit has held that an organization was a limited purpose public figure based not only on the fact of extensive aggressive advertising but upon a "direct relationship between the promotional message and

---

[9] The Third Circuit has refused to extend the principle to cases involving defamatory advertisements by competitors. *See U.S. Healthcare, Inc. v. Blue Cross of Greater Phila.*, 898 F.2d 914, 938–39 (3d Cir. 1990). There, two health-care companies engaged in negative comparative advertising. *Id.* at 917–20. The court noted that "[u]nder traditional defamation analysis, the parties' considerable access to the media and their voluntary entry into a controversy are strong indicia that they are limited purpose public figures." *Id.* at 938. But the court noted that *Steaks Unlimited* "involved a consumer reporter's statement, not a comparative advertising campaign." *Id.* at 938 n.29. Such statements merited stronger protection than commercial advertising, which was "chill-resistant" and not designed to air issues of public concern. *Id.* at 938–39.

the subsequent defamation (indicating plaintiff's pre-existing involvement in the particular matter of public concern and controversy)." *Blue Ridge Bank v. Veribanc, Inc.*, 866 F.2d 681, 687 (4th Cir. 1989) (describing *Nat'l Found. for Cancer Research, Inc. v. Council of Better Bus. Bureaus, Inc. (NFCR)*, 705 F.2d 98 (4th Cir. 1983)).

Here, as in *Steaks Unlimited* and in *NFCR*, Trump University conducted an aggressive advertising campaign in which it made controversial claims about its products and services. This campaign included online, social media, local and national newspaper, and radio advertisements for free introductory seminars. Claims of legitimacy were also propounded in the Foreword to *Trump 101*.[10] The Foreword to *Wealth Building 101* specifically denied that Trump University engaged in the practices that were the target of Makaeff's allegedly defamatory statements.[11] This entire advertising campaign makes Trump University a limited public figure for purposes of the controversy that arose about the legitimacy of its educational practices because its extensive advertising efforts "invited public attention, comment, and criticism." *Steaks Unlimited, Inc.*, 623 F.2d at 274. Moreover, there is a "direct relationship" between

---

[10] For instance, it asserts that Donald Trump is "dedicated to education," and that Trump's "direct insights, experiences, and practical know-how [will] guide" Trump University students "throughout" their experience. Sexton, *Foreword* to *Trump 101*, at xiv.

[11] In it, Sexton notes that some organizations "hook you on promises and never deliver," and, moreover, that "just when you begin to realize that the advice you paid for is unproven and ineffective—they try to sell you more expensive products." Sexton, *Foreword* to *Wealth Building 101*, at ix. He promises, "Neither I nor our chairman, Donald J. Trump, would stand for that at Trump University." *Id.*

Trump University's promotional messages and Makaeff's allegedly defamatory statements, which reflects Trump University's pre-existing involvement in this particular matter of public concern and controversy. *See Blue Ridge Bank*, 866 F.2d at 687; *see also Gilbert*, 53 Cal. Rptr. 3d at 762 ("[T]he alleged defamation must be germane to the plaintiff's participation in the controversy." (quoting *Ampex Corp. v. Cargle*, 128 Cal. App. 4th 1569, 1577 (2005)). We hold that under these circumstances Trump University is a limited purpose public figure with respect to the subject of its advertising.

We reject Trump University's argument, based on the reasoning of the California Supreme Court in *Vegod Corp. v. American Broadcasting Cos.*, 603 P.2d 14 (Cal. 1979), that aggressive advertising of a message addressing a public controversy cannot render an entity a limited public figure. In *Vegod*, two firms sued for defamation over a television news report criticizing the firms' business practices in conducting a close-out sale for a respected but bankrupt department store, the City of Paris, the closing of which had generated a public controversy given the store's landmark status. *Id.* at 15. The California Supreme Court held that the plaintiffs were not limited public figures. *Id.* at 17. It reasoned that while the close-out firms had conducted aggressive advertising, their advertising standing alone did not render them public figures. Noting that "[i]t does not appear that plaintiffs urged City of Paris publicly or otherwise to terminate business or to destroy the 'landmark,'" the court concluded that the advertising had not thrust the plaintiff firms into the vortex of the controversy. *Id.* "Merely doing business with parties to a public controversy does not elevate one to public figure status." *Id.*

Vegod is distinguishable. There, the plaintiffs' close-out advertising did not address the controversy over the planned destruction of the landmark store, and thus the firms were not limited public figures for purposes of that controversy. *Id.* There was no nexus between the critical news reports and the controversial destruction of the store. *See Gilbert*, 53 Cal. Rptr. 3d at 762. Here, Trump University's advertisements, including Sexton's statements, both directly and indirectly address the subject of Trump University's educational practices. Trump University therefore became a limited public figure in the context of the controversy over those practices. Moreover, the limited public figure analysis is not a matter of state substantive law, but rather a pure constitutional question. *See Gertz*, 418 U.S. at 332–35 (discussing the "constitutional privilege" established by *New York Times Co. v. Sullivan*, 376 U.S. 254 (1964)). We are simply not bound by California decisions on this issue.[12]

To be clear: Trump University is not a public figure because Donald Trump is famous and controversial. Nor is Trump University a public figure because it utilized Donald

---

[12] Subsequent decisions by lower California courts appear to have extracted from *Vegod* an inflexible rule that advertising never constitutes "thrusting oneself into the vortex of a controversy." *Rancho La Costa, Inc. v. Superior Court*, 106 Cal. App. 3d 646, 661 (1980) ("The holding of *Vegod* sufficiently answers that advertising is not thrusting oneself into the vortex of a controversy."); *see also Hufstedler, Kaus & Ettinger v. Superior Court*, 42 Cal. App. 4th 55, 70 (1996) (citing *Vegod* and *Rancho La Costa* for the proposition that, in a libel suit, the plaintiff bank's "advertisements themselves could not have been sufficient to transform the Bank into a public figure"). We believe these subsequent cases misread *Vegod*; we do not read *Vegod* to have opined either so broadly or so rigidly. In any event, we are not bound by California state decisions because whether Trump University is a limited public figure is a question determined under federal constitutional law.

Trump as a celebrity pitchman. Trump University is a limited public figure because a public debate existed regarding its aggressively advertised educational practices. Did Trump's famous moniker draw public attention when Trump University's business practices proved worthy of debate? Perhaps. However, having traded heavily on the name and fame of its founder and chairman, Trump University was in no position to complain if the public's interest in Trump fueled the flames of the legitimate controversy that its business practices engendered.

c.

The district court concluded that Trump University was not a limited public figure, and thus did not reach the question of actual malice.[13] Because Trump University is a limited purpose public figure, to prevail on its defamation claim it must establish that Makaeff made her statements with "actual malice," i.e., knowledge of their falsity or reckless disregard of their truth. *Gertz*, 418 U.S. at 342. To demonstrate reckless disregard of the truth, Trump University must show by clear and convincing evidence that Makaeff "entertained serious doubts as to the truth" of her statements. *Id.* at 331–32, 334 n.6 (quoting *St. Amant v. Thompson*, 390 U.S.

---

[13] Because a showing of actual malice necessarily depends on the falsity of the statements at issue, the district court may assume the falsity of the statements and proceed directly to the actual malice inquiry. If it concludes that Trump University cannot establish a reasonable probability of proving actual malice, it need not inquire whether the statements were actually false for purposes of ruling on the motion to strike. *Cf. Underwager v. Channel 9 Austl.*, 69 F.3d 361, 368 (9th Cir. 1995) (where the defamation plaintiff-appellant failed to demonstrate the existence of a material dispute about actual malice, the reviewing court need not decide whether he had established a dispute over falsity).

727, 731 (1968)). If Makaeff was simply republishing a third party's allegations, mere proof of her failure to investigate the veracity of such allegations does not establish reckless disregard for the truth. *Id.* at 332. Trump University would then need to show "obvious reasons" to doubt the truthfulness of the original speaker, or the accuracy of his statements. *Harte-Hanks Commc'ns, Inc. v. Connaughton*, 491 U.S. 657, 688 (1989) (quoting *St. Amant*, 390 U.S. at 732).

On appeal Trump University nevertheless argues that Makaeff's early testimonials praising Trump University indirectly prove that she acted with a high degree of awareness of the probable falsity of her later statements.[14] However, it is plausible that Makaeff sincerely believed in Trump University's offerings when she submitted her written and videotaped testimonials. The gist of Makaeff's complaint about Trump University is that it constitutes an elaborate scam. As the recent Ponzi-scheme scandals involving one-time financial luminaries like Bernard Madoff and Allen Stanford demonstrate, victims of con artists often sing the praises of their victimizers until the moment they realize they have been fleeced. Makaeff's initial enthusiasm for Trump University's program is not probative of whether she acted with actual malice.

That Makaeff's initial email to Trump University omitted the complaints of Trump University's alleged conduct that she later published to third parties also proves little. Makaeff's first email to Trump University was a request for

---

[14] While still in the program, Makaeff described Trump University's programs as "amazing" and "excellent" on rating sheets provided by Trump University. Later, in June 2009, she was videotaped at a workshop praising her mentor and saying favorable things about Trump University.

a refund. It is possible that Makaeff chose to take a more conciliatory tone at this early stage of their increasingly acrimonious dialogue in the hopes of getting her money back. Thus, the district court may find that this initial email is consistent both with Makaeff's later, supposedly defamatory statements, and her contemporaneous goal of persuading Trump University to give her a refund.

Trump University further asserts that Makaeff recklessly republished the unverified complaints of anonymous third parties on the Internet. While the Supreme Court in *St. Amant* suggested that a statement "based wholly on an unverified anonymous telephone call" might justify a finding of actual malice, *id.* at 732, the district court may reach the contrary conclusion: that Makaeff's statements were not based wholly on the anonymous Internet postings but were instead based on Makaeff's own educational experience. That Makaeff herself was disenchanted with Trump University may explain why she would not believe that the critical postings of others were "inherently improbable." *Id.* Nor would the circumstances of the Internet postings necessarily give Makaeff obvious reasons to doubt them—the postings were made on an Internet message board that offered no particular benefit to those who published statements criticizing Trump University.

IV.

Because Trump University is a public figure for the limited purpose of the public controversy over the quality of the education it purports to provide, the district court must address the inherently fact-intensive question of whether Trump University has a reasonable probability of proving, by clear and convincing evidence, that Makaeff made her critical statements with actual malice. We therefore **REVERSE** the district court's denial of Makaeff's motion to strike Trump University's counterclaim pursuant to California's anti-SLAPP statute, and **REMAND** for further proceedings consistent with this opinion.

REVERSED; REMANDED.

Chief Judge KOZINSKI, with whom Judge PAEZ joins, concurring:

I join Judge Wardlaw's fine opinion because it faithfully applies our law, as announced in *United States ex rel. Newsham* v. *Lockheed Missiles & Space Co.*, 190 F.3d 963, 973 (9th Cir. 1999), and its progeny. But I believe *Newsham* is wrong and should be reconsidered.

Erie Railroad Co. v. *Tompkins*, 304 U.S. 64 (1938), divided the law applicable to diversity cases into two broad categories. Overruling *Swift* v. *Tyson*, 41 U.S. 1 (1842), it held that state law, rather than federal common law, applies to matters of substance. *Erie*, 304 U.S. at 78–79. But when it comes to procedure, federal law governs. *See Gasperini* v. *Ctr. for Humanities, Inc.*, 518 U.S. 415, 427 & n.7 (1996); *see also Hanna* v. *Plumer*, 380 U.S. 460, 473 (1965) ("*Erie* and its offspring cast no doubt on the long-recognized power of Congress to prescribe housekeeping rules for federal courts . . . .").

In most cases, it's easy enough to tell whether a rule is substantive or procedural. Whether a defendant is liable in tort for a slip-and-fall, or has a Statute of Frauds defense to a contract claim, is controlled by state law. Just as clearly, the time to answer a complaint, the manner in which process is served, the methods and time limits for discovery, and whether the jury must be unanimous are controlled by the Federal Rules of Civil Procedure. The latter is true, even though such procedural rules can affect outcomes and, hence, substantive rights. *See Hanna*, 380 U.S. at 471.

But the distinction between substance and procedure is not always clear-cut. While many rules are easily recognized as falling on one side or the other of the substance/procedure line, there are some close cases that call for a more nuanced analysis. *See, e.g.*, *Shady Grove Orthopedic Assocs., P.A.* v. *Allstate Ins. Co.*, 130 S. Ct. 1431, 1437 (2010); *Gasperini*, 518 U.S. at 428. In *Walker* v. *Armco Steel Corp.*, 446 U.S. 740, 750–51 (1980), for example, the Supreme Court considered the interplay between Federal Rule of Civil Procedure 3 and Oklahoma's statute of limitations. Rule 3 provided then, as it does now, that a civil action is commenced on the date the complaint is filed. *Id.* at 750. In *Walker*, that date was within the state statute of limitations period. *Id.* at 742. Oklahoma law, however, provided that a civil action began, for statute of limitations purposes, only when the summons was served on the defendant. *Id.* at 742–43. If plaintiff filed the complaint at the end of the limitation period, service would still be timely, so long as it occurred no more than sixty days after the filing of the complaint. *Id.* at 743.

Confronted with a state substantive rule (the statute of limitations) and a federal procedural rule fixing the date when a civil action commences, the Court held that there was no conflict because the two rules dealt with different questions. *Id.* at 750–51. The federal rule, the Court noted, set the date for the commencement of the action for the purpose of measuring various time periods internal to the lawsuit. *Id.* at 751. The rule wasn't meant to affect the time when the statute of limitations was tolled by commencement of the lawsuit. *Id.* at 751–53. The latter was a matter of state substantive law. Because the federal procedural rule and the state substantive rule could coexist peaceably within their respective spheres, the Court concluded that each could be given full effect: The state rule would perform the backwards-looking function of determining whether the action was brought within the statute of limitations, whereas the federal rule would determine when the action began for the forward-looking purpose of measuring time periods applicable to the litigation. *Id.* at 750–53.

Significantly, *Walker* considered whether there was a conflict between the state and federal rules only after it determined that the state rule was substantive, because it defined the period that a right created by state law could be enforced. *See id.* at 746, 749–50. At the same time, a broad reading of the federal procedural rule could impinge on the substantive state law right by extending the statute of limitations. This would have led to the "'inequitable administration' of the law" by giving these plaintiffs greater rights than they would have enjoyed in state court, "solely because of the fortuity that there is diversity of citizenship between the litigants." *Id.* at 753 (quoting *Hanna*, 380 U.S. at 468).

Most of *Newsham*'s analysis was devoted to showing that there's no "conflict" between California's anti-SLAPP statute and the Federal Rules of Civil Procedure and, therefore, the two regimes can operate side-by-side in the same lawsuit. But the question of a conflict only arises if the state rule is substantive; state procedural rules have no application in federal court, no matter how little they interfere with the Federal Rules. *Newsham*'s mistake was that it engaged in conflict analysis without first determining whether the state rule is, in fact, substantive.

It's not. The anti-SLAPP statute creates no substantive rights; it merely provides a procedural mechanism for vindicating existing rights. The language of the statute is procedural: Its mainspring is a "special motion to strike"; it contains provisions limiting discovery; it provides for sanctions for parties who bring a non-meritorious suit or motion; the court's ruling on the potential success of plaintiff's claim is not "admissible in evidence at any later stage of the case"; and an order granting or denying the special motion is immediately appealable. *See* Cal. Civ. Proc. Code § 425.16. The statute deals only with the conduct of the lawsuit; it creates no rights independent of existing litigation; and its only purpose is the swift termination of certain lawsuits the legislators believed to be unduly burdensome. It is codified in the state code of civil procedure and the California Supreme Court has characterized it as a "procedural device to screen out meritless claims." *See Kibler* v. *N. Inyo Cnty. Local Hosp. Dist.*, 138 P.3d 193, 198 (Cal. 2006).

Federal courts must ignore state rules of procedure because it is Congress that has plenary authority over the procedures employed in federal court, and this power cannot be trenched upon by the states. *See Erie*, 304 U.S. at 78 ("[T]he law to be applied in any [diversity] case is the law of the State" except for "matters governed by the Federal Constitution or *acts of Congress* . . . ." (emphasis added)); *see also* 28 U.S.C. § 2072. To me, this is the beginning and the end of the analysis. Having determined that the state rule is quintessentially procedural, I would conclude it has no application in federal court.

But *Newsham* is wrong even on its own terms. *Newsham* recognized a "commonality of purpose" between the state law and Federal Rules of Civil Procedure 8, 12 and 56, but shrugged it off because the parties could take advantage of both the Federal Rules and the very similar anti-SLAPP procedures. *See* 190 F.3d at 972–73. This vastly understates the disruption when federal courts apply the California anti-SLAPP statute.

The Federal Rules aren't just a series of disconnected procedural devices. Rather, the Rules provide an integrated program of pre-trial, trial and post-trial procedures designed to ensure "the just, speedy, and inexpensive determination of every action and proceeding." *See* Fed. R. Civ. P. 1. Pre-discovery motions, discovery, summary adjudication and trial follow a logical order and pace so that cases proceed smartly towards final judgment or settlement.

The California anti-SLAPP statute cuts an ugly gash through this orderly process. Designed to extricate certain defendants from the spiderweb of litigation, it enables them to test the factual sufficiency of a plaintiff's case prior to any discovery; it changes the standard for surviving summary judgment by requiring a plaintiff to show a "reasonable probability" that he will prevail, rather than merely a triable issue of fact; it authorizes attorneys' fees against a plaintiff who loses the special motion by a standard far different from that applicable under Federal Rule of Civil Procedure 11; and it gives a defendant who loses the motion to strike the right to an interlocutory appeal, in clear contravention of Supreme

Court admonitions that such appeals are to be entertained only very sparingly because they are so disruptive of the litigation process. *E.g., Digital Equip. Corp.* v. *Desktop Direct, Inc.*, 511 U.S. 863, 868 (1994); *Mohawk Indus., Inc.* v. *Carpenter*, 130 S. Ct. 599, 605 (2009).

We've already recognized that key aspects of this scheme can't possibly coexist with the Federal Rules of Civil Procedure. The Federal Rules contemplate that the sufficiency of a plaintiff's case will be tested prior to discovery only for legal sufficiency. *See* Fed. R. Civ. P. 12. If a plaintiff's case vaults that hurdle, the Federal Rules provide for a period for discovery before defendant can test plaintiff's case for factual sufficiency. *See* Fed. R. Civ. P. 26, 29–37, 56; *Anderson* v. *Liberty Lobby, Inc.*, 477 U.S. 242, 250 n.5 (1986). The Federal Rules don't contemplate that a defendant may get a case dismissed for factual insufficiency while concealing evidence that supports plaintiff's case. *See* 10B Charles Alan Wright, Arthur R. Miller et al., *Federal Practice & Procedure* § 2740 (3d ed. 2012); *see also* Fed. R. Civ. P. 56(d). The California anti-SLAPP statute allows for precisely that.

That's why we held in *Metabolife International, Inc.* v. *Wornick*, 264 F.3d 832, 845 (9th Cir. 2001), that the "discovery-limiting aspects" of the anti-SLAPP statute don't apply in federal court. *See also* Cal. Civ. Proc. Code § 425.16(f)–(g). The Federal Rules, after all, reflect a policy of forcing a defendant to disclose adverse facts before he may challenge plaintiff's case for factual sufficiency. *See* John H. Beisner, *Discovering a Better Way: The Need for Effective Civil Litigation Reform*, 60 Duke L.J. 547, 554–59 (2010).

In reaching this clearly correct conclusion, *Metabolife* decimated the state scheme. The anti-SLAPP statute is designed, first and foremost, to reduce the time and expense certain defendants spend in court upon being sued. *See Wilcox* v. *Superior Court*, 27 Cal. App. 4th 809, 823 (1994), *disapproved of on other grounds by Equilon Enters.* v. *Consumer Cause, Inc.*, 52 P.3d 685, 694 n.5 (Cal. 2002). It accomplishes this by requiring plaintiff to show that there's a "reasonable probability" he'll prevail on his claim before subjecting the defendant to the cost, delay and vexation of discovery. *See Metabolife*, 264 F.3d at 840. *Metabolife* crippled the anti-SLAPP statute by forcing defendants sued in federal court to suffer the slings and arrows of outrageous discovery, pushing back by months or years the time when they can free themselves from litigation. And, of course, giving a plaintiff discovery makes it much more likely that he'll meet the "reasonable probability" of success standard than his counterpart in state court, who must make that showing without first examining defendant's records or deposing defendant's witnesses.

After *Metabolife*, the federal court special motion is a far different (and tamer) animal than its state-court cousin. *Metabolife* diminished some of the tension between the state and federal schemes, but at the expense of depriving the state scheme of its key feature: giving defendants a quick and painless exit from the litigation. What we're left with after *Metabolife* is a hybrid procedure where neither the Federal Rules nor the state anti-SLAPP statute operate as designed.

From the federal perspective, *Metabolife* left in place quite a bit of disruption: the burden on the plaintiffs to show that they have not merely a triable issue of fact, but a reasonable probability of success; enhanced sanctions for bringing a weak claim; and the cost, disruption and delay inherent in a right to interlocutory appeal—created by state law, rather than by Congress. I find it passing strange that state legislatures have now displaced Congress as the delimiters of our jurisdiction. *See Batzel* v. *Smith*, 333 F.3d 1018, 1024–26 (9th Cir. 2003) (we must allow immediate appeal because of text and legislative history of California's anti-SLAPP statute).

Newsham was a big mistake. Two other circuits have foolishly followed it. *See Godin* v. *Schencks*, 629 F.3d 79, 81, 85–91 (1st Cir. 2010); *Henry* v. *Lake Charles Am. Press, L.L.C.*, 566 F.3d 164, 168–69 (5th Cir. 2009). I've read their opinions and find them no more persuasive than *Newsham* itself. It's time we led the way back out of the wilderness. Federal courts have no business applying exotic state procedural rules which, of necessity, disrupt the comprehensive scheme embodied in the Federal Rules, our jurisdictional statutes and Supreme Court interpretations thereof. As a three-judge panel, *Metabolife* could only do so much, and we are generally bound to follow *Newsham*. But if this or another case were taken en banc, we could take a fresh look at the question. I believe we should.

Judge PAEZ, with whom Chief Judge KOZINSKI joins, concurring:

I concur fully in Judge Wardlaw's fine opinion. I also join Chief Judge Kozinski's concurrence because I, too, believe that *United States ex rel. Newsham v. Lockheed Missiles & Space Co.*, 190 F.3d 963 (9th Cir. 1999), is wrong and should be reconsidered. I agree that California's anti-SLAPP statute is "quintessentially procedural," and its application in federal court has created a hybrid mess that now resembles neither the Federal Rules nor the original state statute.

Yet another reason to reconsider the application of state anti-SLAPP statutes in federal court is that there are significant state-by-state variations within the circuit, despite facial similarities and identical procedural purposes of each state's anti-SLAPP statute. *Newsham*'s holding—although considering only California's anti-SLAPP statute—has been extended to Oregon's anti-SLAPP statute and, arguably, *sub silentio* to Nevada's as well. *See Metabolic Research, Inc. v. Ferrell*, 693 F.3d 795, 798–800, 798 n.4 (9th Cir. 2012) (holding that the denial of a motion to strike under Nevada's anti-SLAPP statute is not an appealable collateral order but not deciding whether "the Nevada anti-SLAPP statute is available to litigants proceeding in federal court"); *Gardner v. Martino*, 563 F.3d 981, 991 (9th Cir. 2009) (holding that Oregon's anti-SLAPP statute, which requires entry of a judgment of dismissal without prejudice, is applicable in federal court because it "does not directly conflict with the Federal Rules and Oregon's civil procedure rules"); *see also Englert v. MacDonell*, 551 F.3d 1099, 1102 (9th Cir. 2009) (dismissing for lack of jurisdiction an appeal from the denial of an Oregon defendant's special motion to strike because the motion functions like a denial of a motion for summary judgment without deciding whether the Oregon statute would conflict with Federal Rule of Civil Procedure 56(c)), *superseded by statute*, Act of June 23, 2009, ch. 449, § 1, 2009 Or. Laws 1194, 1194 (codified at Or. Rev. Stat. § 31.150(1)), *see also id.* § 3, 2009 Or. Laws at 1195 (codified at Or. Stat. § 31.152(4)) (stating that the purpose of the revised anti-SLAPP statute is "to provide a defendant with the right not to proceed to trial in cases in which the plaintiff does not meet the burden specified" by the statute).

These differences play out in the availability of an appeal under the collateral order doctrine. *See DC Comics v. Pac. Pictures Corp.*, 706 F.3d 1009, 1016 (9th Cir. 2013). *DC Comics* recognized that Nevada's statute and Oregon's pre-2010 statute "were more akin to defenses against liability than immunities from suit, in that they did not provide for any consistent right of immediate appeal from the denial of an anti-SLAPP motion." *Id.* It is not the mere availability of immediate state appeal provided in the statute that creates the right to appeal under the federal collateral order doctrine, but rather that when "a legislature provide[s] an appeal unique to its anti-SLAPP statute . . . it could be inferred that its purpose was to confer immunity from suit—an immunity which can only be vindicated by permitting an interlocutory appeal." *Englert*, 551 F.3d at 1107 (discussing the holding in *Batzel v. Smith*, 333 F.3d 1018, 1025 (9th Cir. 2003) that California's immediate appeal provision and the statute's legislative history were instructive in "demonstrat[ing] that California lawmakers wanted to protect speakers from the trial itself rather than merely from liability"). That different state procedures are *already* interpreted by our case law to create ultimately different federal procedural outcomes—such as the availability of appeal under the collateral order doctrine—is further evidence that it makes no sense to treat state anti-SLAPP statutes as substantive state law under *Erie*.